Richard's APE:
Accidental Poems of Extinction

Patrick Pearson

Rewilding Path Publishing

Copyright © 2019 Patrick John Pearson
ISBN: 9781079471991

DEDICATION

This little book is dedicated to all those people who are working to prevent the further loss of wild species from the Earth.

Richard's APE:
Accidental Poems of Extinction

Introduction

What was it like to experience at close hand a dramatic battle between two aurochs bulls 15,000 years ago in the prehistoric marshes which are now the coastline of Wales? We don't know, because they're extinct.

To watch a pair of woolly rhinoceroses mating less than a mile from where Lyme Regis stands today? We don't know, because they're extinct.

To come across an Irish elk helplessly mired in a bog thousands of years before Ireland was separated from the mainland? We don't know, because they're extinct.

To be awed by the unexpected emergence right before our eyes, from a hawthorn wood above what is now Loch Ness, of one of the last straight-tusked elephants to walk the earth? We don't know, because they're extinct.

Kailu, a Palaeolithic cave artist, does know, because he's experienced all of these and more while the species still exist. This little volume contains fifteen sonnets that Kailu would have written if Kailu could write, set within the landscapes that eventually become the British Isles, with each sonnet recounting a meeting between the cave artist and an iconic animal species which humankind later exterminates.

Kailu is a character from my novel *Rewilding Richard*, and the poems of his experiences as he crosses the icy westernmost lands of the untamed European continent appear fully-formed in the notebook of the protagonist of the novel's title. Richard, who has flown from Australia to Britain to 'rewild' himself in landscapes being ecologically restored, is flabbergasted to discover the poems in his own handwriting and can't recall writing any of them.

These fifteen sonnets are a reminder of the tsunami of hundreds and thousands of extinctions occurring worldwide in our Anthropocene age, and a cry for humans of the 21st century to set aside half of Earth's surface for wildness, to give our remaining wild species a chance of survival and our threatened planet the capacity to heal itself.

Sonnets don't have to be fourteen lines. Some of these sonnets take inspiration from master-sonneteers of the past and have twenty lines, or ten, and rhyme, or not. Rules in poetry are meant to be broken, just as in life, even when it appals the rule-bound most.

Accompanying each sonnet there is a brief note about the animal we have lost, and a quick life lesson for humans from its life or its death.

Patrick Pearson

Too fast for a seal, it banked white, veered black through the water

Too fast for a seal, it banked white, veered black through the
water,
Then shot from the sea to where I fished from my snowy ledge;
Slim stubby wings, one of those great auks I'd seen in summer
Far off the coast, on the great sea-rock with their single egg,
Thousands, with that same grooved bill, though with white
spots above their eyes;
This bird was white-striped eye to eye, showed grey feathers
eye to ear,
But gurgled their distinct rock-pillared anxious sound, and I
Knew it wore a winter coat, like the mink and stoat and hare –
Then it dived again below the waves, and time passed, much
time;
I thought it must be lost, taken, till it and another
Arrowed to my ledge from the sea, clacking their bills, crying,
Crooning, beaks inside showing white, like new-mushroom
colour,
Not yellow as in summer – unchanged, quite, were the irises

Of their eyes, so dark, so rich and smooth, like soft chestnut

gyres.

Too fast for a seal, it banked white, veered black through the water is a poem celebrating the great auk, and is written in Shakespearean sonnet form – the most familiar sonnet form for English-speaking readers, developed not by Shakespeare but by Wyatt and Surrey. The fourteen lines of the Petrarchan sonnet become one stanza of three quatrains with a concluding couplet. I have used loose heptameter as meter, roughly fourteen syllables per line, rather than the Shakespearean sonnet's more usual pentameter.

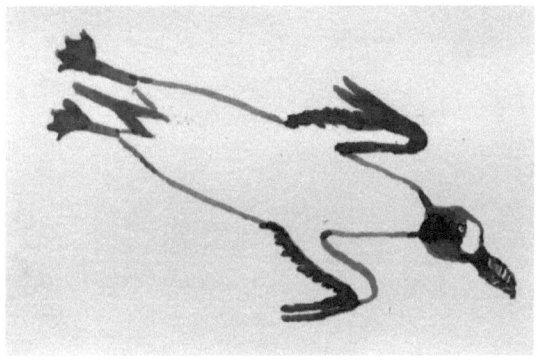

This sonnet confirms the underwater abilities of the great auk (Pinguinus impennis), which could hold its breath for longer than seals are able to. Kailu the cave-artist is delighted to discover how the bird's colours have changed dramatically from summer, when he first encountered thousands of great auks far out to sea on a great sea-stack off the coast of what is now Scotland, to these two winter birds on their annual migration which could take them thousands of miles south of where he meets them in what becomes Cornwall. The volta or turn of thought in the poem comes when the artist-poet realises that the beauty of their eyes remains unchanged.

Great auks were a source of food, feathers, museum specimens, and eggs for collectors. The last great auk in Britain was beaten to death in 1840 by three men from St Kilda, who believed it was a witch, while the last breeding pair of great auks worldwide was strangled to death in 1844 on Eldey off the coast of Iceland by egg collectors, as the great auk's eggs were worth a great deal of money.

Life lesson: The great auk was apparently quite unafraid of humans, who used the auks for horrific ends, including treating live birds as fatty fuel for the fires to cook their fellows. Don't be too trusting of those who end up in positions of power over you, over the country, and over the planet, because many of them have never thought much of long-term consequence at all. Hold them especially to environmental account, so you and others don't end up cooked by climate changes or beaten to death by despair.

The giant deer is already so near death

The giant deer is already so near death,

Held tight by the bog, that I need not fear

The beast's power – his sole intent is breath,

Not to rake those great antlers at me, nor rear

Up – though I have seen men's heads split in two

By those daggered pans wider than my height;

This fen would eat me, sucks at my snowshoes,

Yet I cannot will the deer this slow fate –

Nor pull him free, his weight being triple-bound

To the mire – I can, though, smooth his crossing

To the spirit world, slice his throat, and sound

Out a love-song of his kinfolk to him:

Brother, I shall cave-paint you alive forever,

Your fat will light my lamps, your blood bind my colour.

The giant deer is already so near death, about the Irish elk, is also in Shakespearean sonnet form and is written in loose iambic pentameter.

I haven't modified the structure of the Shakespearean sonnet at all for this sonnet, and the typical appeal or change of tone in a Shakespearean concluding couplet is employed here also. The meter in the couplet changes to iambic hexameter ('alexandrines') for two lines.

The Palaeolithic artist Kailu comes across a giant Irish elk (Megaloceros giganteus giganteus) trapped in a bog in what is now Exmoor. These massive animals were once widespread from Ireland to Siberia. The last of the Irish elk – which was really a huge species of deer, one of the largest ever recorded, with a twelve-foot span of antlers and the weight of ten men – died around 7000 years ago, although there is some speculation that they may have survived in the Siberian tundra into historical times. The cave artist can help the Irish elk to die a merciful death, and then use parts of the deer to immortalise it in his cave-painting.

Did humankind cause the end of the Irish elk? Of course we did. We have been spectacularly successful at wiping out the biggest animals and birds the earth has seen, partly because the energy required for gigantism causes big wild species to procreate slowly –

too slowly to counteract the effects of widespread hunting by an aggressive and expansionist new species. The Irish elk favoured meadows and open woodlands as its preferred grazing territories, and it would have been rather easy to hunt.

Life lesson: The Irish elk probably acquired such huge and massively heavy antlers to impress the opposite sex. Carrying the antlers required substantial energy input for the deer to grow to such a large size, which contributed to its extinction at the hands of humans. A caution to us all is that our energy needs may yet kill off the entire earth unless we have a rethink. As a personal life lesson, don't you go to such lengths to impress the opposite sex, or anyone for that matter, or it may be the death of you. If the girls or boys aren't impressed with the antlers you have, tell them to nick off. Someone out there will like the way you look, and they won't want to cook and eat you.

This entire day I have watched five beavers

This entire day I have watched five beavers

Building a dam from sticks and logs and mud;

I have marvelled at their stocky joy in work,

Their easy grace in water, how they leave

All heaviness behind and flow, log-wood

Clamped between blade-like teeth tanned red by bark.

Two kits, rapt with gnawing and nibbling birch,

Come close to my hide; I see their webbed hind feet

And count the ten slim fingers that grasp their food;

The lake, then, these trees, the beavers, I, converge –

All connect, and meld, and meet.

This entire day I have watched five beavers is a curtal sonnet, a shortened sonnet form devised by Gerard Manley Hopkins ('Glory be to God for Dappled Things'). This one uses loose iambic hexameter, or roughly twelve syllables per line.

Eurasian beavers (Castor fiber) became extinct in Britain in 1526, during the reign of Henry VIII, and we nearly lost the species entirely from Europe and the world. Beavers were almost hunted to extinction for fur and castoreum, so that by 1900, only around a thousand survived in Europe and Asia. It didn't help that the medieval Church regarded the meat of beavers as fish (because the animal spends so much time in water) meaning that beaver-fish meat could be eaten during Lent, and on Fridays, without annoying the Lord.

Now, thankfully, they are being reintroduced to many of the places they once called home, and some of those places are in Britain. In Scotland, they have been recognised as a native species; in England, insanely, that has not yet happened. There are some reintroduced beavers as a research programme in the River Otter in Devon, however, where this Palaeolithic poem is sited. Dam-building beavers are a keystone species – their presence stimulates other beneficial wild species and natural processes, and they modify and improve habitats they find, even improving the quality of the water in the streams they build their lodges in.

Life lesson: The world desperately needs keystone species either reintroduced or encouraged to thrive to help humans repair the environmental destruction wrought so far, so see what you can do to facilitate this. On a personal note, be the beaver of your immediate environment and your community. Choose a career and way of life that is of benefit to others, so that your hard work sustains them even as it simultaneously ensures that you thrive.

The hyena lies dead, skull mashed open

The hyena lies dead, skull mashed open

By hoof or horn of bison or aurochs,

Fearsome object of the clan's wild cries at dawn

When they gave mortal chase – even men walk

Carefully when we hear their whooping call

To hunt; the tarpan on which they preyed is gone,

Fierce horned beasts have come, and hyena fall

Broken now like this spotted yellow one,

Which its clan won't eat, nor drag its dead

Kin carcass down to their bone-soaked sea-cave.

So, I sketch its lifeless figure from head

To toe in charcoal lines that note and save

The strangeness before me – the creature's teats

Leak milk, so it has lately suckled young,

Yet between its legs lie a long penis

And balls, and I am moved to wondering:

This penised female with balls at her tail

May be instead a teated, milk-dugged male.

The hyena lies dead, skull mashed open, set in the Cattedown Caves in Plymouth, is a stretched Shakespearean sonnet, with an extra quatrain taking the sonnet to eighteen lines. A syllabic rhythm of ten syllables per line is used rather than strict iambic pentameter.

The cave hyena (Crocuta crocuta spelaea), also called the Ice Age spotted hyena, preyed on large mammals, especially the primitive wild horse called the tarpan, and accumulated large stockpiles of mammal bones in caves along rivers and the coast. Cave hyena bones have been found as far south as the limestone caves in Plymouth and as far north as Yorkshire. As the steppe vegetation changed to forested woodlands when Europe warmed, the hyenas' diet had to change and they would have hunted bison and aurochs, both more dangerous prey than tarpan. Cave hyena disappeared from Western Europe between 14,000-11,000 years ago, when the grassy lowlands began to shift vegetation type to woodland – or were flooded.

The Palaeolithic artist in this sonnet is correct in thinking that there is something strange with the genitalia of the cave hyena. It would have shared this feature with present-day African spotted hyena females, although it was a much larger animal. African hyena females have a long 'pseudo-penis' through which they give birth, a greatly elongated clitoris almost identical to the male hyena's penis, and they even have the 'balls' that the artist observes.

Life lesson: Not even the greatest courage and tenacity can substitute for ready adaptability. The hyenas, courageous enough to prey upon even bison and woolly rhinoceros and sufficiently tenacious to outcompete cave lion and wolf packs didn't adapt fast enough to survive as a species. If change comes to your environment (natural or otherwise), change faster than your competition.

I search the flinty cliff for colours, for paints

I search the flinty cliff for colours, for paints

That hide in plain view – the black mudstones

That encase spiral shell-rocks like the cones

From pinewood, when burned and crushed, gift ox-blood

stains;

The soft white clay-stone yields dark ochre grains,

Though sometimes dries bright yellow for no known

Reason – above me, close, I hear deep grunts,

And think wild boar, or galloping tarpan;

Instead, I see rhinoceros: immense

Double-horned bull mounting one great cow

Whose coarse-wool coat tatters grey-brown now

That Spring's breath melts the ice: What gentleness

Their broad lips display, how artfully each

Shagged beast dances tender-rough on three-toed feet.

I search the flinty cliff for colours, for paints, about the woolly rhinoceros, is an Italian sonnet in iambic pentameter. The Italian sonnet is an English variation on the traditional Petrarchan sonnet. It keeps the fourteen lines of the Petrarchan sonnet, and the rhyme scheme of its octave, but its sestet rhymes differently and ends with a rhyming couplet.

The woolly rhinoceros (Coelodonta antiquitatis) was bigger than any rhinos we have at present. They were common throughout Europe and survived the last glacial period – and then we killed them off. There are now only five species of rhino left in the world, three of which are critically endangered.

Kailu's Palaeolithic encounter with the two woolly rhinos takes place on the Jurassic Coast of Devon and less than a mile from where Lyme Regis stands today, where he's hunting along the sea-cliff for minerals and rocks from which to craft his prehistoric paint pigments. It's rather ironic that visitors to the Jurassic Coast, probing for fossils from millions of years ago as evidence of life before us, usually have no idea that only a few thousand years ago giant rhinos roamed the area.

Rhinos are faster than you might think. Don't try to outrun a rhino. When they run at their fastest, unbelievably, they run on their toes, and they reach speeds of thirty miles per hour (the very fastest humans can't go faster than about twenty-eight miles per hour and can't sustain that for more than a hundred-metre sprint).

Life lesson: Collectively, let's see what we can do to keep the last three species of a sixty-million-year-old evolutionary miracle alive until the madness of humans' strange affair with rhino horn is over. Personal life lesson: If you really, really need to do something, don't delay it, do it fast, and stay on your toes until it's done.

I entered the cave with care, fearing the toothed cat

I entered the cave with care, fearing the toothed cat, or worse,

Hyena, so moved with quiet, tallow light in my hand,

Feeling the cave's vibrations and the lines of its walls; ice

Shrouded the first cavern, bats the second; the third (and last,

I thought – no air breathed softly from its neck) held pillars, shapes,

Cold flows of lime-rock from floor to arched height; I stood silent

In the vault, then saw the great bear and thought it lay asleep,

And dread filled me – I watched its chest, which stayed as still as death,

Until I was certain, and knelt to touch its icy pelt.

Dead, it was still bigger than all bears I had seen in life;

Here was the lost bear grandfather knew, that wintered in caves,

Its head too broad, thighs over-long, short claws, but fearsome teeth:

Even so, how closely it looked like a tall man in furs –

Give him gloves, shoes, and a hood, he would stroll

unchallenged by.

I entered the cave with care, fearing the toothed cat, about the cave bear and set in the limestone Mendip Hills of Somerset, is a free-verse sonnet written entirely in 'fourteeners', or lines containing fourteen syllables. Free verse poetry is composed of non-metrical, non-rhyming lines that closely follow the natural rhythms of speech. This sonnet keeps nevertheless to a constraining number of syllables per line.

Cave bears (Ursus spelaeus) were larger than the brown bear of today's Europe. Brown bears, the same species as North America's grizzly bears, displaced the cave bear species, probably because brown bears were more versatile in the sites they chose for hibernation. Homo sapiens (us) and Neanderthals would have been competing with cave bears to occupy caves, and cave bears didn't hibernate anywhere but in caves, which made it easier for humans first to displace and then to exterminate them.

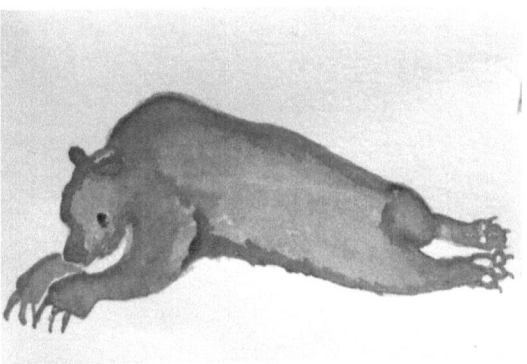

Cave bears were either herbivorous or, if they were indeed omnivores, nevertheless ate mostly vegetarian diets, but they were still dangerous and ferocious – if they were attacked in their caves by the splendidly huge cave lion, very often the lion died in the attack and left its bones as evidence. It seems that cave bears became extinct in Europe and Asia sometime between 24000 and 15000 years ago, so Kailu may never have seen a live cave bear – perhaps why he gets such a fright in this poem.

Life lesson: Both environmentally and socially, the pace of change is increasing. Life is going to demand that you are capable of embracing change when you have to. Don't be too choosy or picky, the way the cave bears were about where they slept at night. Being overly choosy can leave you with too few options to thrive or even survive. You don't want to be like the cave bear and end up hibernating out in the open in winter because all you could conceive of was a cave. Adapt. Make something else work for you.

I worked in silence at the cliff's base

I worked in silence at the cliff's base,

Because the bull was near, guarding his cows,

Magnificent in his muscled wildness,

White eel stripe snowline down his charcoal back,

Proud bull-king to his chestnut harem-herd

Grazing sedge-shoots with his calves by the stream;

Then, at sunset – my pouch only one-third

Filled with shining flakes like dragonflies' wings –

The other bull came, and I and the king

Could read the jet strength, judge the young bull's size:

Taller at the shoulder, his chest as broad

As the king's, smooth flanks yet unscarred by lions,

Great belly and balls, princely horns thrust high.

They fell to, as the sun blazed out in fire,

They drowned the darkening swish of the sea

With the bellowing crash of horns on horns,

And though I could not see its red, the reek

Of blood from each torn gash cloyed in my mouth,

On and on till it was done, and quiet

As death, but for the rasping of one bull's breath.

The sonnet **I worked in silence at the cliff's base**, about watching two aurochs bulls battle for supremacy near where the town of Goldcliff is found now in Wales, is a half-rhymed caudate sonnet in loose iambic pentameter. A caudate sonnet is an expanded sonnet, consisting of fourteen lines in a standard sonnet form followed by a 'coda' – from the Latin *cauda* meaning 'tail'. The coda is a second sestet tacked onto the first, giving the sonnet a total length of twenty lines.

The aurochs (Bos taurus primigenius) was a magnificent and massive species of grazing cattle. Aurochs would ignore humans walking among them, but if they suspected they were being hunted, they would immediately become highly aggressive. What contributed most to their extinction was that their grazing grounds were increasingly occupied as growing human populations brought domesticated cattle into the lower-lying regions of Europe. Eventually, when aurochs were restricted to the forests around Poland it became a death-penalty offence to hunt or poach them. The last aurochs, a female, died in the Jaktorów forest in Poland in 1627. There are ongoing attempts to recreate a species that in some ways resembles and behaves like the aurochs, but the true aurochs is gone, leaving its most lasting impressions in the numerous cave paintings which show how common it was in Stone Age times.

Kailu's search for mica flakes for his pigments from a sea-cliff next to a swamp means he is perfectly placed to witness the titanic battle between rival aurochs bulls, which were much larger and darker than aurochs females and sported a distinctive eel-stripe along the ridge of their backs.

Life lesson, both for humankind and personally: Dr Seuss says that you've a brain in your head, and feet in your shoes, so you can take yourself wherever you choose. That's good advice. If your environment (physical or social) becomes hostile to you and your best efforts cannot change it for the better, move to where circumstances allow you to thrive. The aurochs didn't have that option, but we as individual humans do.

All seemed mist-still in the frozen wood

All seemed mist-still in the frozen wood, when sudden

Drumbeats thundered near me, and a dozen tarpan

Flowed through my clearing as a strong stream washes

Through a storm-built dam – they are like steam-breathed

spirits,

These silent forest forms, whose dun coats would conceal

Their presence from man or bear and wolf – our tarpan

Here are darker than their grassy cousins to the east,

Yet even so they fall easy prey to beasts or flinted arrows –

I'll show through paint their graded blends of colour, their

Shadowed necks, their coal-drawn stripes or shimmering spots

That sometimes shine from sun-warmed skins, their silhouettes

Of frizzy manes and heads too big for their small eyes,

Small ears, small stocky bodies: Their numbers fall so,

It seems their time is done or – somehow – yet to come.

All seemed mist-still in the frozen wood, about a herd of tarpan in forest where Weybridge is situated now, is written as a free-verse sonnet, although it employs an octave-sestet form and a twelve-syllable metrical line, alexandrine-like, throughout.

Tarpan, or Equus ferus ferus, the European primitive wild horse, may have become extinct in the British Isles about 9000 years ago, when forest regrew over the steppe grassland that had formed when the last glacial period ended. A stocky wild horse with tarpan-like features is recorded as surviving in the highlands of Britain and in western Europe, however, even into the eighteenth century, and tarpan remained present in Eurasia until the very first years of the twentieth century, although there is some speculation that these 'tarpan' were in fact hybrids of true wild horses and feral domesticated horses.

Tarpan were a favourite prey of many of the predators that roamed Europe after the retreat of the ice masses, but their extinction was human-caused. In historical times, wild horse meat formed a ready source of protein for numerous cultures, and humans simply grew too numerous for the herds of wild horses to survive. In the Americas, no horses at all survived the arrival of humans.

What Kailu records in his sonnet is meeting a herd of tarpan that has adapted to living in the forests that are beginning to replace the southern steppes, and how various their coat colours are. Even 15,000 years ago, he would have realised that their numbers were declining, and that as a wild species, at least, their days were numbered.

Life lesson: Tarpan disappeared as domestic horses increased in number. Yet the tarpan seems latent in domestic horses, which show great facility in becoming feral and thriving as feral herds, given the opportunity, so that each generation becomes more truly wild. Environmentally, free-roaming wild horses play a vital role in restoring degraded habitats, which is a cause to support. As a personal life lesson, be adaptable, as horses are, and look for your opportunities to live life according to your own rules. And when you find them – take them as a strong stream washes through a storm-built dam.

Just before the autumn dawn, we step lightly over the new snow

Just before the autumn dawn, we step lightly over the new
snow
To where the silent trees approach the Mystery, the great stone
Ring
Whose wet sarsen stones whisper that a harsh winter is to
follow;
The lintel-stones glow softly redder now, with the sun rising,
And each cut block becomes salmon flesh; I stroke my bow,
loop its string,
Then thrill, as the Circle starts to hum, giant stones warming to
the light –
Close by, we hear the warning bark of roe, deep, a hidden buck
flagging
Its alarm. I nock an arrow, and touch my child's arm, for quiet.

Instantly the sarsen explodes into spotted black and beige and
white,
And a deer catapults up, across, down, in an arc before us

So lightning-fast I cannot comprehend at first its cause: A

bright-

Eyed lynx, crouched low with the neck of the doe clamped tight

between its jaws –

I am certain though that I saw no spoor in the snow, no prints

on the ground;

Our lynx would have lain patient all still night upon its rock,

uttered no sound.

Just before the autumn dawn, we step lightly over the new snow, about the lynx, is a Spenserian sonnet. The Spenserian sonnet is a fourteen-line poem developed by Edmund Spenser in his *Amoretti*, that varies the English or Shakespearean sonnet form by interlocking the rhyming of the three quatrains. This sonnet is written in loose iambic octameter, roughly equivalent to sixteen syllables per line, with the meter altering to eighteen syllables per line for the rhyming couplet of the sestet.

Of the four lynx species worldwide, the Eurasian lynx (Lynx lynx) is the largest, and it is presently the third largest predator in Europe, after the brown bear and the grey wolf. The lynx is very much a forest predator, and roe deer is its favourite prey species. The lynx was still present in Britain until very recently – around 700 years ago, or even later. As lynx never attack humans and seldom prey upon sheep, there is (hooray!) a gathering movement to return the lynx to Britain.

Even Kailu is unused to encountering lynx, because they are one of the most secretive and elusive of all the cats, and this lynx he 'sees' at Stonehenge is experienced while he is in a visionary trance. His vision takes place in the Bronze Age when Stonehenge is built, ten thousand years after his journey across the British landscape.

Life lesson: The lynx survived so long in Britain by avoiding humans and human settlement. It's a stealth hunter and takes its prey by surprise. There are at least two lessons here for all of us. One, you'll be a happier and more authentic you if you get away from humans and human settlements frequently; and two, if you're on the hunt towards a vital goal, keep as silent about it as you can and prepare with absolute precision before you launch your (metaphorical) attack.

The bison crashed over the falls, fell from the cloudless morning sky

The bison crashed over the falls, fell from the cloudless
morning sky
Onto my wraith-pool rocks, setting the ducks to flight, while I
in fright
Watched as its chaser, a great wolf with fur as black as starless
night,
Tore out its throat, then called to his pack with howling full-
throated cry;
I marvelled at his broad-ruffed mane, his expressive gold-
amber eyes;
He glanced at me, then, careless, free, as his mate – snow to his
jet, white-
Furred and green-eyed, with two pups, legs over-tall and eyes
yellow-bright –
Leaped the icy slopes to rip red flesh from the bison's steaming
sides.

These long-coated wolves must have come from the vast ice-
mountained north-east,

Must be newcomers, because fearless at this pool they break
their fast;

The black male – father – looks my way again, scours the heart
from the beast,

Then retreats, as do his pack; each secure on strips of wintry
frost:

I would share in your kill, life-brother, prey being scarce save
for your bison feast,

And I long to see a time when all warring between men and
wolves has passed.

The bison crashed over the falls, fell from the cloudless morning sky, set at Pwll-y-Wrach in the Brecon Beacons, is a Petrarchan sonnet of fourteen lines and employs an unusual syllabic metre of sixteen syllables per line (approximating iambic octameter) for the entire sonnet, except for the final two lines, which each contain eighteen syllables.

The Eurasian or grey wolf (Canis lupus lupus) can be pure white to almost jet black, and is a social animal, travelling in nuclear families consisting of a monogamous mated pair and the pair's adult offspring. Although humans domesticated wolves many millennia ago, and even though attacks by wolves upon people are extremely rare, they have been persecuted by humans for aeons, so that the Eurasian wolf was very nearly lost entirely. The last English wolf was killed in the early sixteenth century, while in Scotland they lasted until the great Scottish forests were burned, and the last Scottish wolf was killed in 1684. Wolves are a vital keystone species, and although reintroductions are underway in Europe, no plans exist as yet to bring them back into Britain, where their presence would be immensely beneficial environmentally.

Kailu realises with joy that the great wolves he has met don't share the fear of humans that the wolves of the more peopled south-west display, which is why he believes they must be from the north-east.

Life lesson: A small group of very vocal and passionate (in this case, wolf-) haters, thinking only short-term, can sway entire populations to ignore the truth, the facts, and moral decency. Humans are unfortunately susceptible to persuasion if someone stokes their fears, politically, environmentally or socially. Don't allow fickle public opinion to sway your individual judgement on any matter of substance. Be passionate for the truth and for doing the right thing, especially with an eye on long-term consequences.

The white-blazed throat tells me he is back

The white-blazed throat tells me he is back from his long lusty

summer circuit, my wolverine of the missing toe, whose

limp does not slow his graceless gait, for he quickly runs down

hare and weasel; his female here will after Autumn dig

her snow-banked den, and only late in Spring will young

appear.

A kit from last year's litter trails him – same bear-like paws

and light flank-stripes over dark-haired rump, though more

silver in

his almost-otter face – they squat and stream foul paste on

rocks,

needlessly, for no other male has been here in years, but

it may be they scent the spirit-piss of long-dead rivals.

I am surprised by his kit – he has always kept alone;

perhaps he senses death, wants his seed a fuse to survive –

no tenderness, unless when he mates, though his female must

share his insane fearlessness which makes lone bears and

wolves walk

wide round voracious wolverine carnage: I watch these two

strip a still-iced elk-haunch of stone-hard sinew, crack and

break

the bones, and then crunch to bits the frozen hooves; after they

lope

away at last, not even splinters lie upon the snow.

The white-blazed throat tells me he is back, about seeing a male wolverine and its kit in the area where Cambridge is now, is a contemporary free-verse sonnet, although the usual fourteen lines are stretched to eighteen. A décima of ten lines takes the place of the octave, an octave replaces the sestet, and the sonnet concludes with a chiming couplet. Each line is composed of fourteen syllables, so the sonnet is made up of eighteen 'fourteeners'.

The wolverine (Gulo gulo gulo) became extinct in the British Isles around 8000 years ago but survives still in the boreal forests and subarctic and alpine tundra of northern Europe. It is ferocious and strong quite out of proportion to its size (the size of a medium dog), and often kills prey many times larger than itself. There is a documented case of a wolverine killing a polar bear by latching onto its throat and suffocating it to death. Wolverines have special molars that are reversed ninety degrees, and they use these to break through bone. Their powerful jaws and special molars allow them to eat every part of an animal –including the bones, hooves and teeth. Why was it made extinct in Britain? Its coat is legendary for being hydrophobic. The wolverine's hairs resist water to an astounding degree, making its fur valuable to trappers.

The cave artist recognises that the adult male in the poem is returning from a wide roaming. Male wolverines have vast roaming ranges which include the territory of six or seven females.

Life lesson: Be bold. Be fearless. Don't be cowed by bullies of any sort. As Nelson advised, 'The boldest are the safest'. Confront enemies without fear and they'll be confused at your courage. That's to your advantage. Oh, and another lesson from the wolverine, for the world and for each of us: Don't waste food.

Concealed, I watch boar forage at winter's ending

Concealed, I watch boar forage at winter's ending,

Stripping berries from the vines by the stream, rooting

Bulbs and tubers from the hard soil; the night-dark

Male furrows trenches this way and that while the coarse-

Bristled sows and striped-velvet squeakers trail his hump-

Necked mass, sniff out the ballistic leavings of his

Bladed snout, his axe-shaped head that rams the rigid ground

And flings black mounds of rocks and earth into the air.

The boar scoops worms, frogs, an adder – is bitten thrice;

Untroubled, dices it with tusks and hoof and gulps

It down – how silent his force, while the sows grunt their

Deep-throat delight at each new find, and the sucklings

Squeal like tinkling ice. I feel his dark deadly might;

One *Ukh! Ukh! Ukh!* and I shall trust my heels in flight.

Concealed, I watch boar forage at winter's ending is a free-verse sonnet of fourteen lines, with a distinct octave and sestet. The poem is unrhymed except for the final couplet, although internal rhyme and chime is employed. Metrical length is, for the most part, twelve syllables per line.

Wild boar have developed the ability to be impervious to snake venom, like the mongoose, honey badger, and hedgehog. The main predator of wild boar are grey wolves, though they mainly take piglets and young boar, rarely attack adult sows, and almost completely avoid adult males, because the male boar is quick and dangerous. The original wild boar of the British Isles (Sus scrofa) was probably already extinct at the hands of humans by the thirteenth century, in William Wallace and Edward I's time, and attempts to reintroduce them from stock in Europe failed to create strong and stable wild populations. Now, however, the wild boar has found its way back into Britain in numerous locations (including the Forest of Dean, the area where Kailu watches this little family) – descendants of escapees from wild boar farms with an admixture from feral domestic pigs.

The association between humans and boar goes a long way back, as pigs were being domesticated from wild boar around 15,000 years ago in the Near East, roughly the same time as Kailu is watching these boar foraging in the wood.

Life lesson: One, concerning snakes and other dangerous animals – humans aren't immune to snakebite venom, but we're only likely to be bitten by a snake if we try to harm it or corner it. Leave them alone and they, like most wild creatures, hasten to get away from us. Two, concerning each of us and our choices – if you're a domestic pig, you're going to be eaten. If you're a wild boar, there is at least a chance that you'll live a free life and raise your family as a wild boar should. In modern human society, it's unlikely you'll be *given* the chance of living a free life – you'll have to *decide* on living a free life.

The mammoth glows stark white against the reeds

The mammoth glows stark white against the reeds,

His snowy hair, unmoulted still, reflects

The sun; he will not need long hair this Spring,

Must have come far, because his tusks are smoothed

Beneath, from where he's pushed the ice aside

To graze; rare mammoth, solitary bull

Whose hump stands twice my height and means he need

Not fear the lion, nor the wolf – although

In truth, one too-small ear is almost halved,

A patch of rump is bald and scarred, his cone-

Shaped head and shambling back are oddly wrong,

Because I feel the shape of elephants is true,

His tusks are likewise curved too tight; it seems

The mammoth draws towards an endless night.

The mammoth glows stark white against the reeds, about a
woolly mammoth in what becomes the Midlands, is a blank verse
sonnet consisting of fourteen lines made up of an eight-line octave
followed by a six-line sestet. Blank verse is unrhymed and is almost
always in iambic pentameter. The 'volta' or turn of thought in this
sonnet occurs in the middle of the eighth line – the Palaeolithic
artist who meets the snow-white mammoth at first sees only its
great strength and power, but then realises that it is more
vulnerable than at first sight, especially as he sees it during a brief
warm phase that hints at warmer times to come. The mammoth
represents a species whose time on earth seems to be ending,
giving way to successors more suited to the climatic future.

The mammoth (Mammuthus primigenius) is the third-most
represented animal in Palaeolithic cave-art. Our cave-artist's albino
mammoth glows so brightly partly because of the many oil glands
secreting oils into the mammoth's long hair, which kept it warm
and waterproof even in the foulest weather and climate.

Life lesson: Surely the mammoth's great strength and dominance
of its environment should have kept the species safe? Surely, Earth
is so big that human activities cannot really devastate it? The world
is just as vulnerable as were the mammoths to 'death by a thousand

cuts'. Be determined to look beyond the seemingly obvious and foresee the cumulative outcome of multiple injuries or assaults – for yourself, for those you love, and for all things living.

Below the sea of pine, new oak and thorn

Below the sea of pine, new oak and thorn,

Still-unnamed Loch Ness sparkles in its glen;

The elephant cow, as tall as three men,

Domed bulk hidden by the thick hawthorn wall,

Pushes smooth white tusks like great ivory

Needles through the branching boughs, long shafts

As straight as poles to their end-curved tips, tusks

To frame that trunk which grasps and shears the spiked stems.

I hold my flint-headed spear motionless,

Hands dry, held breath as still as certain death

Should she sense me where I crouch unseen –

I have never felt before such power,

Presence; she knows I am here, weighs my fear,

Even foretells her end-song by my Being –

Yet the matriarch with the long straight tusks

Moves on into deeper, darker hedge;

My insubstantial body drops dead down,

And I lie a long while so, in silence,

Before I move too, back into the

Coming world, the whittling world of men.

Below the sea of pine, new oak and thorn, about seeing a straight-tusked elephant near the melting glacier forming Loch Ness, is an unrhymed caudate sonnet in loose iambic pentameter, or lines of five metrical feet, closely conforming to ten syllables per line. The coda used here is six lines, like a second sestet tacked onto the first, giving the sonnet a total of twenty lines.

The magnificent straight-tusked elephant (Palaeoloxodon antiquus), which became extinct in Europe about 10,000 years ago, once had a territory which included Scotland, though its date of extinction in the British Isles may have been many years earlier than its European extinction. Elephants' rough browsing would have contributed to the emergence of coppicing plants such as hawthorn. The biggest animals have been hardest hit by the rise of humankind. There were once many different species of elephant, but now only three species remain: The African bush elephant, the African forest elephant, and the Asiatic elephant.

Kailu meets the straight-tusked elephant cow in the thorny woods colonising the thawing hills around Abriachan, alongside Loch Ness, during a warming period before the area freezes over again, and long before the great Caledonian forest would cover the entire Scottish landscape.

Life lesson: Elephants have high intelligence and they also demonstrate high levels of empathy, which for millennia humans have regarded as a trait only possessed by us. It seems, however, that elephants outstrip humankind in the empathy department, and we can learn from them. Have empathy for all things living, and as you live your life, minimise the hurt and harm you cause other living things – whether animals or trees or fellow humans. Everything hurts. Help them where and when you can.

Running mammoth draw my gaze to the floor

Running mammoth draw my gaze to the floor

Of the valley, and I see beasts in life

Which I've only seen on cave-walls before;

My heart drums with joy, though limbs prick with fright

And make me grateful for my cliff-topped height

Above the fleeing crash pursued by cats

Beige like lions – yet leaner, and in bright

Daylight, and sprinting swift as eagle-shot –

Closer now, their fur betrays remnant spots

Like once-dark paint washed faint by years of sleet,

Their tails seem short; their mouths, by all the gods,

Hold blades, sharp down-curved tusks where should be teeth:

How strange we are – though beauty, art, may thrill us

We hold most regard for things that would kill us.

Running mammoth draw my gaze to the floor, about scimitar toothed cats, is a Spenserian sonnet with three interlocking quatrains giving fewer differently-rhymed line-endings than for example in a Shakespearean sonnet. This sonnet is mostly iambic pentameter, although the rhythm and likewise the meter shift often to avoid the poem's becoming sing-song.

The scimitar toothed cat (Homotherium latidens), about the same size as today's African lion, but with spots and much shorter tails, was once widespread throughout Europe and Asia. Estimates of its date of extinction have changed from 300,000 years ago to 30,000 years ago. It's possible they survived later but that the evidence of their presence is buried underwater, as they were lowland plains predators. They evolved and adapted for open grassland running: They had shorter claws than most cats, longer, slenderer limbs suggesting they hunted in groups during the day, longer snouts with larger nasal openings for faster intake of breath at speed, and long incisor teeth for slashing the jugular of big plains animals like mammoths. As humankind moved into the plains areas and hunted out most of the prey the scimitar toothed cats depended upon, they were ill-adapted to move into woodland, so would have declined sharply in numbers until the species was under threat – and then gone.

In this poem, our Palaeolithic poet observes, from the safety of a cliff, rarely-seen scimitar toothed cats chasing a group of mammoths, which I've called a 'crash', the same collective noun for rhinos, across the low valleys which eventually become the English Channel.

Life lesson: Be adaptable. Has this lesson come up before? The scimitar toothed cat was built for the plains and could not easily adapt to another environment, but we humans can survive and thrive anywhere. The major impediment to our quick adaptation is always in our own mindsets. Collectively, humanity desperately needs to adapt our lifestyles to do less harm to the planet. Individually and personally as humans, the lesson from the cats is that we remain in charge of our destiny. When you need to be a plains predator, be that. When you need to be a woodland creature, make the move, and make it quickly – before your resources run out.

About Patrick Pearson

I'm a writer, artist and speaker, passionate about 'rewilding' or ecologically restoring half of the earth's surface to combat extinction and stabilise global ecosystems. I'm also fascinated with the place and role of 'extinction poetry' in highlighting the extent of the environmental crisis caused by humankind in the Anthropocene. I spend time especially in Sydney, Cape Town and in Britain, travelling as often as I can to explore the wild beauty of the natural world.

If you enjoyed this little volume you may want to have a look at the novel from which these sonnets sprang.

Find out more about me and the novel *Rewilding Richard* at http://patrickjohnpearson.com/

www.ingramcontent.com/pod-product-compliance
Lightning Source LLC
Chambersburg PA
CBHW020330290526
45785CB00007B/2996